Dartmoor Myths & Legends

Compiled by Robert Hesketh

Bossiney Books

Hound Tor (see opposite page)
The cover photograph is of Brent Tor (see page 4).
The photograph on the title page shows the keep of
Okehampton Castle (see page 18).

First published 2020 by
Bossiney Books Ltd, 67 West Busk Lane, Otley, LS21 3LY
www.bossineybooks.com
ISBN 978-1-906474-85-0

Acknowledgements
All photographs are by the author – www.roberthesketh.co.uk

Printed in Great Britain by R Booth Ltd, Penryn, Cornwall

Introduction

Most of the material for this book was collected in the Victorian era and is drawn from several sources. It is related in the words of the collectors, but lightly edited to avoid excessive detail, archaic words and phrases.

The main sources are:

William Crossing (1847-1928), who devoted much of his life to studying Dartmoor and its people.

Rev. Sabine Baring-Gould (1834-1924), the squire and parson of Lew Trenchard, an eclectic scholar and a prolific writer. Among over 1,200 publications are his collections of folk tales, legends and folk songs.

Mrs Bray (1790-1883), who wrote a series of long and detailed letters in the 1830s describing western Dartmoor to her friend, the Poet Laureate Robert Southey.

Robert Hunt (1807-1887), a Cornish mineralogist, antiquarian, poet and early pioneer of photography. His folklore collection is mainly Cornish, but also has Devon material.

Hound Tor

From *A Book of Dartmoor* by Sabine Baring Gould

Hound Tor is a noble mass of rocks. It derives its name from the shape of the blocks on the summit that have been weathered into forms resembling the heads of dogs, peering over the natural battlements and listening to the merry call of the horn.

Satan versus King Arthur

From *Folklore and Legends of Dartmoor* by William Crossing

The deeds of Satan while 'going to and fro the earth' and 'walking up and down in it,' invariably reveal him in conflict with man, though he is usually very careful to hide his real intentions and let it appear as though he desired to help him. Whether this was the case when he once encountered a powerful adversary on the hills above the gorge of the Teign we have been unable to discover, for the story merely tells us of a conflict, and says nothing about what led to it. His antagonist, no less a personage than the redoubtable

King Arthur, seems to have given him as good as he sent, for when Satan, mounting a lofty height, commenced to fling quoits at the British king, he speedily found himself assailed in a similar manner.

Arthur took his stand on another hill about a mile distant, and from its summit discharged his missiles with terrible effect. As the quoits fell, they became changed into masses of rock, and these may still be seen. Their number is considerable, and we may therefore conclude not only that the engagement lasted some time, but also that it was of a desperate character. But eventually Satan found that he had met with his match and was glad to beat a retreat, leaving Arthur triumphant. The hill on which the king took his stand is situated near the road leading from Moretonhampstead to Bridford, and is known as Blackystone or Blackingstone. The enemy had entrenched himself on Hel Tor, further to the north. This name simply implies height, and is found, often in compound, in many places.

Satan and Brentor Church

From *Folklore and Legends of Dartmoor* by William Crossing

It is not to be supposed that Satan is fond of church-going, but he visits them sometimes. In a church in Cornwall a small door used formerly to be opened during baptisms in order that when renounced the fiend might readily make his departure. This was called the Devil's door, and was on the north side of the church. That is the quarter favoured by evil spirits, and thus everything was made as convenient as possible for him.

His presence in these sacred edifices is usually due to a desire to work mischief, and so rooted is his antipathy to them that he has been known to endeavour to prevent the building of them. The churches of Brent Tor, Buckfastleigh and Plympton furnish instances of this. The first named was intended to be built at the foot of the lofty peak which it now crowns. But the builders had not proceeded far with their work when they were surprised on arriving at the scene of their labours one morning to find that the stones they had already placed in position had been removed. A diligent search was made for them, and at length they were discovered on the summit of the hill. They were brought down, and the work of building recommenced.

When the men ceased their labour parts of the walls had again risen a foot or two above the ground, and though hardly supposing that they would be thrown down again, it was not with entire absence of misgiving that they went to their homes. That night, when those who possessed clocks and happened to be awake, heard them strike the hour of twelve, a tall, dark figure approached the site of the intended church. With a contemptuous gesture he raised his foot, and with a few powerful kicks levelled the work of the builders. Then, with equal expedition, he conveyed the stones to the top of the conical hill which he had determined should be the site of the church. His power was not sufficient to enable him to stop the building of it altogether, but he had some control over the work, and was determined that if there was to be a church it should be placed in a situation difficult of access, by which he hoped very few would ever attend it.

Once more the workmen arrived on the spot where they had laid their foundations, but not a stone was to be seen. They guessed now where they should find them, and it was not long before they were brought from the tor a second time. But they might have spared themselves the trouble of removing them, for their indefatigable foe that night again conveyed them to the summit of the crag that crested the hill. This was several times repeated, and then it became plain to the labourers that Satan had set himself against them. As they recognised they were no match for the Devil, it was decided that they must let him have his way, and so it was agreed that they should erect the church on the tor.

The Black Rider

From *A Book of the West* by Sabine Baring Gould

There existed formerly a belief on Dartmoor that it was hunted over at night in storm by a black sportsman, with black fire-breathing hounds, called the 'Wish Hounds.' They could be heard in full cry, and occasionally the blast of the hunter's horn on stormy nights.

One night a moorman was riding home from Widecombe.

There had been a fair there; he had made money, and had taken something to keep out the cold, for the night promised to be one of tempest. He started on his homeward way. The moon shone out occasionally between the whirling masses of thick vapour. The horse knew the way better perhaps than his master. The rider had traversed the great ridge of Hameldon, and was mounting a moor on which stands a circle of upright stones – reputedly a Druid circle, and said to dance on Christmas Eve – when he heard a sound that startled him – a horn, and then past him swept without sound of footfall a pack of black dogs.

The moorman was not frightened – he had taken in too much Dutch courage for that – and when a minute after the black hunter came up, he shouted to him, 'Hey! Huntsman, what sport? Give us some of your game.'

'Take that,' answered the hunter, and flung him something which the man caught and held in his arm. Then the mysterious rider passed on. An hour elapsed before the moorman reached his home. As he had jogged on he had wondered what sort of game he had been given. It was too large for a hare, too small for a deer. Provokingly, not once since the encounter had the moon flashed forth. Now that he was at his door he swung himself from his horse, and still carrying the game, shouted for a lantern.

The light was brought. With one hand the fellow took it, then raised it to throw a ray on that which he held in his arm – the game hunted and won by the Black Rider. It was his own baby, dead and cold. This story was told by the blacksmith at Moretonhampstead to G P Bidder, the calculating boy, who as a lad was fond of playing about the old man's forge. From one of Mr Bidder's daughters I had the tale.

The Legend of Tamara

From *Sacred Texts* by Robert Hunt

The lovely nymph Tamara was born in a cavern. Although her parents were spirits of the earth, the child loved the light of day. Often had they chided her for yielding to her desires and visiting the upper world; and often had they warned her against the consequences which would probably arise from her neglect of their advice.

The giants of the moors were to be feared; and it was from these that the earth spirits desired to protect their child.

Tamara – beautiful, young, heedless – never lost an opportunity of looking on the glorious sun. Two sons of Dartmoor giants – Tavy and Tawrage – had seen the fair maid, and longed to possess her. Long was their toil, and the wild maiden often led them over mountain and moor in playful chase.

Under a bush in Morwenstow, one day, both Tavy and Tawrage came upon Tamara. They resolved now to compel her to declare upon which of them her choice should fall. The young men used every persuasion, and called her by every endearing name. Her parents had missed Tamara, and they sought and found her seated between the sons of the giants whom they hated. The gnome father caused a deep sleep to fall on the eyes of Tavy and Tawrage, and then he endeavoured to persuade his daughter to return to his subterranean cell.

Tamara would not leave her lovers. In his rage the gnome cursed his daughter, and, by the might of his curse, changed her into a river, which should flow on for ever to the salt sea. The lovely Tamara dissolved in tears, and as a crystal stream of exceeding beauty the waters glided onward to the ocean.

At length Tavy awoke. His Tamara was gone; he fled to his father in the hills. The giant knew of the metamorphosis, and, to ease the anguish of his son, he transformed him into a stream. Rushing over rocks, running through morasses, gliding along valleys, and murmuring amidst the groves, Tavy still goes on seeking for Tamara – his only joy being that he runs by her side, and that, mingling their waters, they glide together to the eternal sea.

Tawrage awakened after a long sleep. He divined what had taken place, and fled to the hills to an enchanter. At his prayer he, too, was changed to a stream; but he mistook the road along which Tamara had gone, and onward, ever sorrowing, he flows – away – away – away from his Tamara for ever.

Thus originated the rivers, the Tamar, the Tavy, and the Taw.

A Top Hat in the Mire

From *A Book of Dartmoor* by Sabine Baring Gould

There is a story told of one of the nastiest of mires on Dartmoor, that of Aune Head. A mire, by the way, is a peculiarly watery bog, that lies at the head of a river. It is its cradle, and a bog is distributed indiscriminately anywhere.

A mire cannot always be traversed in safety; much depends on the season. After a dry summer it is possible to tread where it would be death in winter or after a dropping summer.

A man is said to have been making his way through Aune Mire when he came on a top-hat reposing, brim downwards, on the sedge. He gave it a kick, whereupon a voice called out from beneath, 'What be you a-doin' to my 'at?'

The man replied, 'Be there now a chap under'n?' 'Ees, I reckon,' was the reply, 'and a hoss under me likewise.'

There is a track through Aune Head Mire that can be taken with safety by one who knows it.

Tavistock Abbey and its Foundation by Ordulf

From *A Book of the West* by Sabine Baring Gould

The legend, as told in a cartulary summarised in Dugdale's *Monasticon*, is that, in the reign of Edgar, Ordulf was one night praying in the open air, when he saw a pillar of fire brighter than the sun at noon hovering where now anyone, on any day, may see a lowering cloud of smoke. That same night an angel bade him go forth at dawn and explore the spot where he had seen the fire, and then build an oratory to the four evangelists.

I think I can explain the vision. The farmer was 'swaling.' At a certain period a good many pillars of fire may be seen about Tavistock, when either the furze is being burnt, or the farmers are consuming the 'stroil'– the weeds from their fields. So I do not reject the story as altogether fabulous, but as 'improved.'

What Ordulf had a mind to do was to establish a monastery for the comfort of his soul, having, I doubt not, bullied and maltreated the poor Britons without compunction. His father had had a mind the same way, but had died without performing what was his intent.

Next day Ordulf went to the spot where he had seen the fire, and there beheld four stakes, marking out the ground, and this fact confirms me in my opinion. For it was the custom of the natives thus to indicate the bounds of their fields. The stakes were called *termons*. In like manner miners indicated their setts by cutting four turves annually at the limits of their grounds.

Ordulf now set to work and erected an oratory with buildings for an abbot and brethren, and he gave them of his inheritance Tavistock, Milton, Hatherleigh, Burrington, Rumonsleigh, Linkinhorne, Dunethem, and Chuvelin, which I cannot identify. He also bestowed on the monastery his wife's dower.

When the monastic church was built he moved to it the bones of his father, mother, and brother, and after his death was there laid himself.

A Feline Sacrifice

From *A Book of Dartmoor* by Sabine Baring Gould

A story associated with Lustleigh church has its parallels elsewhere. After it had been built the devil threatened to destroy it, stained glass and all, unless he were given a sacrifice. Now it happened that a bumpkin was present in the churchyard with a pack of cards in his pocket, and the Evil One immediately demanded him as his due; but the man, with great presence of mind, pounced on a cat that was stalking by and dashed out its brains against the wall of the porch. This satisfied the powers of darkness, and the consecration of the church followed.

The story is a clumsy late cooking up of the old belief that before a building could be occupied a life must be sacrificed to the telluric deities. A horse, a dog, a sow – in this case a cat was offered up. Echoes of the same are found everywhere. Most Devonshire churchyards were formerly supposed to be haunted by some animal or other, which had been buried under the cornerstone.

Bishop Bronescombe meets Satan

From *A Book of Dartmoor* by Sabine Baring Gould

Walter Bronescombe was Bishop of Exeter between 1258 and 1280, and he lies buried in the Cathedral under a fine canopied tomb. The effigy is of his own date, and gives apparently a true portrait of a worthy prelate.

One day he was visiting this portion of his diocese, and had ventured to ride over the moor from Widecombe. He and his retinue had laboured through bogs, and almost despaired of reaching the confines of the wilderness. Moreover, on attaining Amicombe Hill they knew not which way to take, for the bogs there are nasty; and his attendants dispersed to seek a way. The Bishop was overcome with fatigue, and was starving. He turned to his chaplain and said, 'Our Master in the wilderness was offered by Satan bread made of stones. If he were now to make the same offer to me, I doubt if I should have the Christian fortitude to refuse.'

'Ah!' sighed the chaplain, 'and a hunk of cheese as well!'

'Bread and cheese I could not hold out against,' said the Bishop.

Hardly had he spoken before a moorman rose up from a peat dyke and drew nigh; he had a wallet on his back.

'Master!' called the chaplain, 'dost thou chance to have a snack of meat with thee?'

'Ay, verily,' replied the moorman, and approached, hobbling, for he was apparently lame. 'I have with me bread and cheese, naught else.'

'Give it us, my son,' said the Bishop; 'I will well repay thee.'

'Nay,' replied the stranger, 'I be no son of thine. And I ask no reward save that thou descend from thy steed, doff thy cap, and salute me with the title of master.'

'I will do that,' said the Bishop, and alighted.

Then the strange man produced a loaf and a large piece of cheese.

Now, the Bishop was about to take off his cap and address the moorman in a tone of entreaty and by the title of master, when the chaplain perceived that the man had one foot like that of a goat. He instantly cried out to God, and signified what he saw to the prelate,

10

who, in holy horror, made the sign of the cross, and lo! the moor-man vanished, and the bread and cheese remained, transformed to stone.

Do you doubt it? Go and see. Look on the Ordnance Survey map and you will find Bread and Cheese marked there. Only Bronescombe's name has been transformed to Brandescombe.

But the Bishop, to make atonement, and to ease his conscience for having so nearly yielded to temptation, spent great sums on the rebuilding of his cathedral.

[On the OS map this is now 'Branscombe's Loaf' at SX552891.]

The Legend of Grey Wethers Stone Circle

From *Folklore and Legends of Dartmoor* by William Crossing

Grey Wethers, according to a story I gathered in the neighbour-hood many years ago, were once boys, who had made their way to this remote spot on the slope below Sittaford Tor for the purpose of 'playing ball', though what the game actually was I could not discover. This, in itself is, of course, innocent enough, but unfor-tunately they chose the wrong day. They went to play on a Sunday, and were punished by being turned into stone.

A similar fate befell some men who also went forth to enjoy themselves on what should have been their day of rest and in this case it is probable that, like the youths, they engaged in dancing. They chose a hill near the headwaters of the Wella Brook for their sports, and we may presume that all went well for a time. Then suddenly their revels were brought to an end, and in the place of a gay company only senseless lumps of granite dotted the sward. The event is commemorated in the name of the hill, which is called Pupers, a corruption, it is supposed, of pipers, and these, together with the merrymakers, may still be seen. It is noticeable that in these stories the punishment inflicted is death, as in the case of the man 'that gathered sticks on the Sabbath day,' as related in the Book of Numbers.

Childe the Hunter

From *A Book of Dartmoor* by Sabine Baring Gould

A certain Childe, a hunter, lost his way in winter in Dartmoor's wilderness. Snow fell thick and his horse could go no further.

> In darkness blind, he could not find
> Where he escape might gain,
> Long time he tried, no track espied,
> His labours all in vain.

> 'His knife he drew, his horse he slew
> As on the ground it lay;
> He cut full deep, therein to creep,
> And tarry till the day.

> The winds did blow, fast fell the snow,
> And darker grew the night,
> Then well he wot he hope might not
> Again to see the light.

> So with his finger dipp'd in blood,
> He scrabbled on the stones –
> 'This is my will, God it fulfil,
> And buried be my bones.

> 'Whoe'er it be that findeth me,
> And brings me to a grave;
> The lands that now to me belong
> In Plymstock he shall have.'

The story goes on to say that when the monks of Buckfast heard of this they made ready to transport the body to their monastery. But the monks of Tavistock were beforehand with them; they threw a bridge over the Tavy, ever after called Guile Bridge, and carried the dead Childe to their abbey. Thenceforth they possessed the Plymstock estate.

The kistvaen is, of course, not Childe's grave, for it is prehistoric, and Childe was not buried there. But the cross may have been set up to mark the spot where he was found.

Childe's Cross was quite perfect, standing on a three-stepped pedestal, till in or about 1812, when it was nearly destroyed by the workmen of a Mr Windeatt, who was building a farmhouse nearby. The stones that composed it have, however, been for the most part recovered, and the cross has been restored as well as might be under the circumstances.

Tolmen and 'Christening'

From *Folklore and Legends of Dartmoor* by William Crossing

In the bed of the North Teign is the oft-visited Tolmen, a large block of stone through which wind, gravel and water have pierced a hole sufficiently large for a man to pass through. A story told in the locality speaks of children having formerly been brought here to be 'christened'. This may be the remains of a tradition showing that the stone was once put to some use in connection with certain ceremonies in which lustration (purification) formed an important part, or it may, which is much more probable, have been fastened upon this stone in recent times in consequence of the older antiquarians speaking of it as a tolmen… Tolmens were once thought to have been resorted to by people troubled with certain diseases, and a superstition of this kind was formerly attached to the Whooping Rock on Easdon Tor, on the common near Manaton and North Bovey. Children were taken there to be cured of the whooping cough; hence the name of the rock.

Elfrida's Story

As told by Sabine Baring Gould in *A Book of the West*

Ordgar, Earl of Devon, was father of the beautiful Elfrida, who accordingly was sister of Ordulf. Her story, though tolerably well known, must not be passed over here.

King Edgar was a little man, but thought a good deal of himself – a merciful dispensation of Providence accorded to little men to make up for their lack of inches. He was of a warm complexion. He once carried off a nun from her convent, and was reprimanded for it by Saint Dunstan, who forbade him for this disreputable act to wear his crown for seven years. His first wife was Ethelfleda, called the Duck – Duckie, doubtless, by her husband – and after her death he looked out for another, as is an infirm way that widowers have.

Edgar, hearing that Elfrida, daughter of Ordgar, was the loveliest woman in England, with a true Devonshire complexion of cream and heather-bloom, sent Ethelwald, Earl of the East Angles, to interview her before he committed himself. Ethelwald no sooner saw her than he was a 'gone coon', and he asked the hand of Elfrida from her brother. Having received his consent, he hurried back to the king and told him that the lady was much over-rated, that her chief beauty lay in her wealth; as her only brother Ordulf was childless, she had expectations of coming in for his fortune when it should please Providence, and so on.

So, as though looking only to her expectations, Ethelwald asked the king to give him the lady. Edgar yielded his consent, and Ethelwald married Elfrida, and became by her the father of a boy whom he persuaded the king to take as his god-child, and to whom he gave the name of Edgar. Then Ethelwald was glad, for he knew that according to the laws of the Church, they had contracted a spiritual relationship which would prevent the king from ever marrying Elfrida and removing himself, the obstacle which stood in the way should he contemplate a union.

Now the report reached the king that he had been 'done', done out of the loveliest woman in Christendom, and the little man ruffled up and became fiery red, and vowed he would a-hunting go, and hunt in the royal chase of Dartmoor. So he sent word to Ethelwald that he purposed visiting him at his castle and solicited a bed and breakfast.

Ethelwald felt uneasy. He told his wife the story of the deception he had practised, which shows how soft and incapable of dealing with women he was. Then he went on to ask of her the impossible – to disguise her beauty. As if any woman would do that!

But when Elfrida knew the story she also ruffled up, not a little, and made a point of dressing herself in her most costly array, braiding her lovely hair with jewels, and washing her pretty face in milk and *eau de*-elder-flowers. Edgar became madly enamoured, and to boot furious with the man who had deceived him. As they were together one day hunting, and were alone, the king smote Ethelwald with a javelin so that he died, and he took Elfrida to be his wife; and to expiate his peccadillo, erected a convent.

Salted Fayther

From *Description of the Part of Devonshire bordering on the Tamar* by Mrs Bray

A traveller attempting to cross the moor at the breaking up of a long frost was overtaken by a great snow storm as night was drawing on. He reached a solitary cottage and asked to be taken in for the night. He found there an old woman and her son, a sturdy peasant, who was smoking his pipe over a great fire. There were but two beds in the cottage, and the son offered to give up his own and sleep on the settle by the fire.

The good dame busied herself in preparing what food the house could afford for the stranger's supper, and at length he retired to rest. Neither the room nor the bedding were such as promised comfort to a person accustomed to the luxuries of life, but as most things derive their value from comparison, so did these mean lodgings.

Before going to rest he had observed in the chamber a large oak chest; it was somewhat curious in form and ornament and had the appearance of being of great antiquity. He made some remarks upon it to the old woman when she had lighted him upstairs, in order to see that all things in his chamber were as comfortable for his repose as circumstances would admit. There was something, he thought, shy and odd about the woman when he remarked on the chest, and after she was gone he had half a mind to take a peep into it, but he forbore and went to bed as fast as he could.

He felt cold and miserable; and who in that condition can ever hope for a sound and refreshing sleep? His was neither the one nor the other, for the woman and the chest haunted him in his dream, and a hollow sound, as if from behind his bed head, started him out of his initial sleep. As he started up in bed, the first thing he saw was the old chest that had troubled him in his dreams. There it lay in the silvery silence of the moonlight, looking cold and white and, as connected with his dream, a provoking and even alarming object of his curiosity. And then he thought of the hollow sound, which had seemed to call him from his repose, and the old woman's odd manner when he had talked to her about the chest, and the reserve of her sturdy son, and in short the traveller's imagination supplied a thousand subjects of terror; indeed so active did it now become that it gave action even to the most inanimate things; for he looked and looked again, till he actually fancied the lid of the chest began to move slowly up before his eyes!

He could endure no more. Starting from his bed, he rushed forward, grasped the lid with trembling hands, and raised it up at once. Who shall speak his feelings when he beheld what that fatal chest now disclosed? – A human corpse, stiff and cold, lay before his sight! So much was he overcome with the horror of his feelings that it was with extreme difficulty that he could once more reach the bed.

How he passed the rest of the night he scarcely remembered; but one thought, one fear, possessed and agonised his whole soul. He was in the house of murderers! He was the next victim! There was no escape; for where, even if he left the chamber, at such an hour in such a night, where should he find shelter on the vast, frozen and desolate moor? He had no arms, he had no means of flight, for if plunder and murder were designed, he would not be allowed to pass out of the house while the young man (now, in his apprehension, a common trafficker in the blood of the helpless) slept in the only room below, and through which he must pass if he stirred from where he was.

To dwell on the thoughts and feelings of the traveller during that night of terror would be an endless task. Rather let me hasten to say that it was with the utmost thankfulness and not without some surprise that he found himself alive and undisturbed by any midnight assassin when the sun at last arose and threw the cheerful light of day across the monotonous desolation of the moor. He determined to hasten away, to pay liberally, but to avoid doing or saying anything to arouse suspicion.

On descending to the kitchen he found the old woman and her son busily employed in preparing no other fate for him than that of a good breakfast; and the son, who the night before was probably tired out with labour (and perhaps not all that pleased at the prospect of a night in the settle) had now lost what the gentleman had fancied to be a surly humour. He gave his guest a country salutation, hoped 'his honour' had found good rest, and proceeded to recommend the breakfast in the true spirit of honest hospitality; particularly praising the broiled bacon, as 'Mother was reckoned to have a particularly good hand at salting 'un in.'

Daylight, civility and broiled bacon the traveller now found to be the most excellent remedies against the terrors, both real and otherwise, of his imagination. The fright had disturbed his nerves, but the keen air of those high regions and the savoury smell of a fine smoking rasher, were great restoratives. Indeed so much did he feel reassured and elevated by the total extinction of all his personal fears that, just as the good woman was broiling him another rasher, he out with the secret of the chest, and let them know that he had been somewhat surprised by its contents, venturing in a friendly tone to ask for an explanation of so remarkable a circumstance.

'Bless your heart, your honour, 'tis nothing at all,' said the young man, ''tis only fayther!'

'Your father!' cried the traveller, 'What do you mean?'

'Why you see, your honour,' replied the peasant, 'the snaw being so thick, and making the roads so cledgey, like, when old fayther died two weeks agon, we couldn't carry 'un to Tavistock to bury 'un; so mother put 'un in the old box, and salted 'un in. Mother's a fine hand at salting 'un in.'

Need more be said of this sensitive traveller and his breakfast?

He now looked with horror at the smoking rasher, and fancied it nothing less than a slice of old fayther. He got up, paid for his lodging, saddled his horse, and quitting the house where surprise, terror, joy and disgust had all by turns so powerfully possessed him, he made his way through every impediment of snow and storm.

Never afterwards could he be prevailed upon to touch bacon.

Sir Francis Drake brings Water to Plymouth

From *The Borders of the Tamar and the Tavy* by Mrs Bray

A story told of this hero is that the people of Plymouth were so destitute of water in the reign of Queen Elizabeth, that they were obliged to send their clothes to Plympton to be washed in fresh water. Sir Francis Drake resolved to rid them of this inconvenience. So he called for his horse, mounted, rode to Dartmoor, and hunted about until he found a very fine spring. Having fixed on one that would suit his purpose, he gave a smart lash to his horse's side, pronouncing as he did so some magical words, when off went the animal as fast as he could gallop, and the stream followed his heels all the way into the town. This assuredly was not only the most wonderful, but the most cheap and expeditious, way of forming a canal ever recorded by tradition.

Lady Mary Howard

From *Devonshire Characters and Strange Events* by Sabine Baring Gould

Lady Howard was a person of strong will and imperious temper, and left a deep and lasting impression on the people of Tavistock. She bore the reputation of having been hard-hearted in her lifetime. For some crime she had committed (nobody knew what), she was said to be doomed to run in the shape of a hound from the gateway of Fitzford to Okehampton Park, between the hours of midnight and cock-crowing, and to return with a single blade of grass in her mouth to the place whence she had started; and this she was to do till every blade was picked, when the world would be at an end.

Dr Jago, the clergyman of Milton Abbot, however, told me that occasionally she was said to ride in a coach of bones up West Street, Tavistock, towards the moor; and an old man of this place told a friend of mine the same story, adding that 'he had seen her scores of times'. A lady also who was once resident here, and whom I met in company, assured me that, happening many years before to pass the old gateway at Fitzford as the church clock struck twelve, in returning from a party, she had herself seen the hound start.

When a child I heard the story, but somewhat varied, that Lady Howard drove nightly from Okehampton Castle to Launceston Castle in a black coach driven by a headless coachman, and preceded by a fire-breathing black hound; that when the coach stopped at a door, there was sure to be a death in that house the same night.

As a fact, Lady Howard did not have a carriage but a Sedan-chair. An inventory of her goods was taken at her death for probate, and this shows that she had no wheeled conveyance. The story of the Death Coach is probably a vague reminiscence of the Goddess of Death travelling over the world collecting human souls.

The White Bird of the Oxenhams

From *Devonshire Characters and Strange Events* by Sabine Baring Gould

The Oxenham family of South Zeal has been remarkable for the tradition of a bird having appeared to several of its members previously to their death. James Howell, who had seen mention of this circumstance on a monument at a stonemason's in Fleet Street, which was about to be sent to Devonshire, gives a copy of the inscription in one of his letters.

This letter, dated July 3, 1632, relates that he saw the monument with the inscription relating the circumstance of the apparition. It appears ... the persons whose names are mentioned in the epitaph all died in the year 1635, three years after the date of his letter. The persons to whom the apparition appeared were John Oxenham, son of James Oxenham, gentleman, of Zeal Monachorum, aged twenty-one, and said to have been six feet and a half in height, who died Sept. 5, 1635, a bird with a white breast having appeared hovering over him two days before; Thomazine, wife of James Oxenham, the younger, who died Sept. 7, 1635, aged twenty-two; Rebecca Oxenham, who died Sept. 9, aged eight years; and Thomazine, a child in the cradle, who died Sept. 15.

It is added that the same bird had appeared to Grace, the grandmother of John Oxenham, who died 1618. It is stated also that the clergyman of the parish had been appointed by the Bishop (Hall) to enquire into the truth of these particulars, and that a monument, made by Edward Marshall, of Fleet Street, had been put up with his approbation, with the names of the witnesses of each apparition.

Widecombe Storm 1638

From *Folklore and Legends of Dartmoor* by William Crossing

Sometimes Satan is charged with having raised a storm in order to bring about the destruction of a church, presumably for the reason that the work being accomplished there interfered with his own... There is more than one tale of great damage having been wrought, and among these the story of the Widecombe storm of 1638 is not the least wonderful. But if moorland tradition be correct this does not appear to have been brought about for the reason above suggested. Satan's visit to the church, and the dreadful storm it occasioned, was for the purpose of claiming as his own one who had bartered his soul for a brief period of worldly enjoyment.

In my youthful days more than one story used to be told of the 'wicked Jan Reynolds', of Widecombe, and of the sad end to which he came. Having entered into a compact with Satan whereby he was to be provided with what money he needed until such time as he should be found in Widecombe Church, when he was to become Satan's prey, he set about 'enjoying himself', which meant indulging in every sort of wickedness.

Jan thought himself secure, for the church was the last place he desired to go. One version of the story has it that Jan was to be discovered asleep in the church; but, however that may be, the day fell when his ghostly enemy became aware that Jan, forgetting himself or being muddled with drink, was at the afternoon service at Widecombe. Mounting his black steed, Satan set out at a gallop for the village, stopping for a brief space at the inn at Pound's Gate in order to refresh himself and enquire the way.

Arriving at the church, he flung himself from his horse and darted towards the porch. Immediately a thick darkness fell, and as he entered the building one of the pinnacles of the tower, struck by lightning, fell bodily onto the roof of the nave, and a terrific peal of thunder awoke the echoes of the valley. Satan strode to the seat in which Jan Reynolds had ensconced himself and seized him by the neck. Then it became apparent what the wretched youth had been engaged in. In his hand were four cards, but though they were aces they were to bring him no more luck. The Devil vaulted into the saddle, and giving his steed the rein the animal mounted into the air and disappeared into the gloom. The cards fell from Jan Reynolds's hand, and ere they reached the ground became transformed into small newtakes. These enclosures may still be seen on the side of the hill near where the West Webburn rises; they bear a rude resemblance in form to the pips on the cards.

Widecombe Fair

Traditional Devon folk song collected by Rev. Sabine Baring Gould

'Tom Pearce, Tom Pearce, lend me your grey mare,
All along, down along, out along, lee.
For I want for to go to Widecombe Fair,
Wi' Bill Brewer, Jan Stewer, Peter Gurney, Peter Davy,
Dan'l Whiddon, Harry Hawk, old Uncle Tom Cobley and all,'
CHORUS: Old Uncle Tom Cobley and all.

'And when shall I see again my grey mare?'
All along, &c.
'By Friday soon, or Saturday noon,
Wi' Bill Brewer, Jan Stewer, &c.'

So they harnessed and bridled the old grey mare.
All along, down along, out along lea.
And off they drove to Widecombe fair,
With Bill Brewer, Jan Stewer, Peter Gurney, Peter Davy,
  Dan'l Whiddon, Harry Hawke,
Old Uncle Tom Cobley and all,
Old Uncle Tom Cobley and all.

Then Friday came, and Saturday noon,
All along, &c.
But Tom Pearce's old mare hath not trotted home,
Wi' Bill Brewer, &c.

So Tom Pearce he got up to the top o' the hill
All along, &c.
And he seed his old mare down a-making her will
Wi' Bill Brewer, &c.

So Tom Pearce's old mare, took sick and her died
All along, &c.
And Tom he sat down on a stone, and he cried
Wi' Bill Brewer, &c.

But this isn't the end o' this shocking affair,
All along, &c.
Nor, though they be dead, of the horrid career
Of Bill Brewer, &c.

When the wind whistles cold on the moor of a night
All along, &c.
Tom Pearce's old mare doth appear, ghastly white,
Wi' Bill Brewer, &c.

And all the long night be heard skirling and groans,
All along, &c.
From Tom Pearce's old mare in her rattling bones,
And from Bill Brewer, Jan Stewer, Peter Gurney, Peter Davy,
Dan'l Whiddon, Harry Hawk, old Uncle Tom Cobley and all.
CHORUS: Old Uncle Tom Cobley and all.

Sir Richard Cabell

In Methuen's *Little Guide on Devonshire* (1907), Sabine Baring-Gould wrote:

Before the south porch of Holy Trinity Church, Buckfastleigh is the enclosed tomb of Richard Cabell of Brooke, who died in 1677. He was the last male of his race, and died with such an evil reputation that he was placed under a heavy stone, and a sort of penthouse was built over that with iron gratings to it to prevent his coming up and haunting the neighbourhood; when he died (the story goes) fiends and black dogs breathing fire raced over Dartmoor and surrounded Brooke, howling.

Stephens' Grave

From *Folklore and Legends of Dartmoor* by William Crossing

On the common above Cudlipp Town, beside a grassy path that leads to the forest at Walkham Head, is a low, grassy mound, which was once said to be haunted by the spirit of a suicide whose grave it marks. A young man of the neighbourhood, having been deceived by the girl to whom he had given his heart was unable to bear the cruel stroke, and rashly took his life. The poor body was denied Christian burial, and was laid in the earth on the open moor, a stake being driven through it to ensure it should not rise again. But though this was effectual so far as the body was concerned it could not keep the spirit from rising, and the people in the neighbourhood soon found it would have been more to their comfort, as it most certainly would have been to their credit, had they caused the body to be decently interred in the churchyard. It was speedily rumoured that the young man's ghost had been seen by the mound, and nobody would pass over the green track after nightfall. How, or when, it was finally laid is unknown, but all in the locality agree that it has never 'walked' within living memory. But the story is not forgotten, and Stephens' Grave may still be seen by the rambler in this part of the moor.

Dolly's Cot

From *A Book of Dartmoor* by Sabine Baring Gould

Proceeding half a mile [from the Dartmeet/Two Bridges road] a ruined cottage is reached, where the stately Yar Tor may be seen to advantage. This ruin is called Dolly's Cot.

Dolly, who has given her name to this ruin, was a somewhat remarkable woman. She lived with her brother, orphans, by Princetown when Sir Thomas Tyrwhitt settled at Tor Royal. She was a remarkably handsome girl, and she seems to have caught the eye of this gentleman, who located her and her brother in the lodge, and then, as the brother kept a sharp look-out on his sister, he got rid of him by obtaining for him an appointment in the House of Lords, where he looked after the lighting, and had as his perquisite the ends of the wax tapers. As fresh candles were provided every day, and the sessions were at times short, the perquisites were worth a good deal.

However, if the brother were away Dolly had another to watch over her, one Tom Trebble, a young and handsome moorman, who did not at all relish the manner in which Sir Thomas, Warden of the Stannaries, hovered about Miss Dolly.

But a climax was reached when the Prince Regent arrived at Tor Royal to visit his forest of Dartmoor. The Prince's eye speedily singled Dolly out, and the blue coat and brass buttons, white ducks tightly strapped, and the curled-brimmed hat were to be seen on the way to Dolly's cottage a little too frequently to please Tom Trebble. So to cut his anxieties short he whisked Dolly on to the pillion of his moor cob and rode off with her to Lydford, where they were married. Then he carried her away to this cottage – now a ruin – on the Dart, to which led no road, hardly a path even, and where she was likely to be out of the way of both the Prince and his humble servant, Sir Thomas.

In this solitary cottage Tom and Dolly lived for many years. She survived her husband, and gained her livelihood by working at the tin-mine of Hexworthy, where one of the shafts recently sunk was named after her.

Dolly lived to an advanced age, and even as an old woman was remarkably handsome and of a distinguished appearance. It is now difficult to collect authentic information concerning her, as only very old people remember Dolly. She was buried at Widecombe, and aged moor folk still speak of her funeral, at which all the women mourners wore white skirts, i.e. their white petticoats without [outside] the coloured skirts of their gowns, and white kerchiefs pinned as crossovers to cover their shoulders.

The distance is between six and seven miles. Dolly was borne to her grave by the tin-miners, and followed not only by the mine-workers, but by all the women of the moorside, and all in their white petticoats; and as they went they sang psalms.

Pixies, a note by William Crossing
From his *Guide to Dartmoor*

The former belief in these little elves was one of the most interesting of the Devonshire superstitions. But their existence is now regarded by the peasantry with something more than doubt. They were said to be the souls of unbaptized children, and though they sometimes appeared as a small bundle of rags, were more often seen in the form of beings dressed in fantastic garments, mostly of a green colour... While sometimes found to be mischievous, they more often evince a desire to aid the industrious housewife or husbandman. Their favourite haunts on Dartmoor were the Pixies Cave on Sheep's Tor, the Piskie's Holt in Huccaby Cleave and New Bridge on the Dart below Holne.

Tavistock pixies

From *Description of the Part of Devonshire bordering on the Tamar* by Mrs Bray

I have not yet said much about our bogs on the moor, which from some luckless horse or other being now and then lost in them, have obtained as their popular name that of the 'Dartmoor stables'. These bogs in old times must have been exceedingly dangerous; even now that we have a road through the moor which displays all the happy results of Mr McAdam's genius, yet nevertheless if a mist suddenly comes on, the stranger feels no small concern for his own safety. Mr Bray assures me that when he used, in early life, to follow up with enthusiasm his researches on the moor, not heeding the weather, he has frequently been suddenly surprised and enveloped in such a dense mist that he could scarcely see the ears of the animal on which he rode. Once or twice he was in some peril by getting on boggy ground, when his horse, more terrified than himself, would shake and tremble in every joint, and become covered in foam from the extreme agony of fear.

If such adventures have now and then happened even in these days, how far more frequently must they have occurred when there was no regular road across the moor! How often a traveller, if he escaped with his life, must have wandered about for hours in such a wilderness before he could fall into any known or beaten track, to lead him from his perils towards the ancient town of Tavistock, or the villages with which it is surrounded!

I mention this because I think there cannot be a doubt that similar distresses gave rise to the popular belief still existing, not only on the moor but throughout all this neighbourhood, that whenever a person loses his way, he is neither more nor less than 'pixy-led'…

The good dames in this part of the world are very particular in sweeping their houses before going to bed, and they frequently place a basin of water by the chimney nook, to be helpful to the pixies, who are great lovers of water; and sometimes the pixies pay back the good deed by dropping a piece of money in the basin. A young woman of our town, who declared she had received the reward of sixpence for a like service, told the circumstance to her gossips; but no sixpence ever came again, and it was generally believed that the pixies had taken offence by her chattering, as they don't like to have their deeds, good or evil, talked over by mortal tongues.

Many a pixy is sent out on works of mischief, to deceive the old nurses and to steal away young children, or to do them harm. Many also, bent on mischief, are sent forth to lead poor travellers astray, to deceive them with those false lights called Will-o'the-wisp, or to guide them in a fine dance in trudging home through woods and waters, through bogs and quagmires and every peril.

Others, who content themselves with a practical joke, and who love frolic more than mischief, will merely make sport by blowing out the candles on a sudden, or kissing the maids 'with a smack', so that they shriek out 'who's this?' – till their grandmothers come and lecture them for allowing unseemly freedoms with young men.

Some are sent out to frolic or make noises in wells; and the more gentle and kindly of the race will spin flax and help their favourite damsels to do their work. I have heard a story about an old woman in this town who suspected she received assistance of this nature, and one evening coming suddenly into the room, she spied a ragged little creature who jumped out at the door. She thought she would try still further to win the services of her elfin friend, and so bought some smart new clothes, as big as those made for a doll. These pretty things she placed by the side of her wheel; the pixy returned and put them on; when, clapping her tiny hands in joy, she was heard to exclaim these lines:

> Pixy fine, pixy gay,
> Pixy now will run away.

And off she went, but the ungrateful little creature never spun for the old woman after.

The wicked and thievish elves, who are all said to be squint-eyed, are despatched on the dreadful errand of changing children in the cradle. In such cases (so say our gossips in Devon) the pixies behave to the stolen child just as the mortal mother may happen to behave towards the changeling dropped in its stead. I have been assured that mothers who credit these idle tales pin their children to their sides in order to secure them; though even this precaution has proved useless, so cunning are the elves. I heard a story not long ago about a woman who lived and died in this town and who most solemnly declared that her mother had a child that was changed by the pixies whilst she, good dame, was busied in hanging out some linen to dry in her garden. She almost broke her heart on discovering the cheat, but took the greatest care of the changeling; which so pleased the pixy mother, that sometime later she returned the stolen child, who was ever after very lucky.

It is reported that in days of old, as well as in the present time, the wild waste of Dartmoor was much haunted by spirits and pixies in every direction; and these frequently left their own lands to exercise their mischievous tricks and gambols even in the town of Tavistock itself – despite the fact that it was then guarded by its stately abbey, well stocked with monks, who made war on the pixy race 'with bell, book and candle' at every opportunity. And it is also alleged that the devil (who if not absolutely the father is, assuredly, the ally of all mischief) gave the pixies his powerful aid in all manner of delusion.

Sometimes he would carry his audacity so far as to enter the venerable abbey grounds, always, however, carefully avoiding the holy water – a thing which would transform him from whatever disguise he was using into his own true shape and person. But the good people here state that these days the clergy are more learned than formerly, and the burial service so much enlarged compared to what it was in earlier days, that the spirits are more closely controlled, and the pixies held tolerably fast, and conjured away to their own domains.

Pixies are said to congregate together, even by their thousands, in some of those wild and desolate places where there is no church. In a field near Down-house, there is a pit which the pixies, not very long ago, appropriated for their ball room. There, in the depths of the night, the owl, who probably stood as sentry for the company, would hoot betweenwhiles; and sounds such as never came from mortal voice or touch would float in the air, whilst the elves would whirl in giddy round.

Whitchurch Down is said to be very famous for the peril of there being pixy-led; for there many an honest yeoman and stout farmer, especially if he should happen to take a cup too much, is very apt to lose his way; and whenever he does so he will declare, and offer to take his Bible oath upon it, 'That as sure as ever he's alive to tell it, whilst his head was running round like a mill-wheel, he heard with his own ears they bits of pisgies, a-laughing and a-tacking their hands, all to see he led astray and never able to find the right road, though he'd travelled it scores of times previous, by night or by day, as a body might tell.'

And many good old folks relate the same thing, and how pisgies delight to lead the aged a-wandering about after dark.

But as most evils set men's wits to work to find out a remedy for them, even so we in this part of the world have worked out our remedies against such tiresome tricks. For whoever finds himself pixy-led, has nothing more to do than to turn jacket, petticoat, pocket or apron inside out, and a pixy, who hates the sight of impropriety in dress, cannot stand this; and off the imp goes, as if he'd been sent packing with a flea in his ear.

Now this turning of jackets, petticoats, etc, being found so good as a remedy, was then tried as a preventive; and as some good mother may now and then be prevailed with to give her darling Doctor Such-a-one's panacea to keep off a disease before it makes an appearance, even so do our good old townsfolk practise this turning inside-out ere they venture on a walk after sundown near any suspected place, as a certain preventive against being led astray by a pixy.

Jan Coo

From *Tales of the Dartmoor Pixies* by William Crossing

At Dartmeet, the two branches of the Dart mingle their water, and the course of the united stream, until it leaves the uplands, is through a deep and narrow valley overhung with rugged tors. An observer from one of the heights crowning the sides of the valley identifies the course of the river, as it rushes along its rocky channel, by the white flashes of foam. The grey granite sides of the tors contrast strikingly with the coppices of oak, and the whole scene is one of great wildness.

On the left bank of the river rises the bold conical pile of Sharp Tor, and on the slope of this hill stands a solitary farmhouse called Rubric [now Rowbrook], overlooking the valley below. At this farm a boy was once employed to tend the cattle – a quite inoffensive lad, who fulfilled his duties to the satisfaction of his master.

One evening in the winter season, when he had been nearly twelve months on the farm, he came hurriedly into the kitchen, exclaiming that he had heard someone calling, and imagined that it must be a person in distress. The farm workers who were gathered around the cheerful peat fire rose quickly, thinking it quite likely that some wayfarer had lost his way in the valley. They quickly reached the spot where the boy said he had heard the voice, and paused to listen.

Nothing but the sound of the rushing river below met their ears, and the men declared that the boy must have been mistaken. He, however, stoutly asserted that he was not, and as if to bear him out, a voice was suddenly heard, seemingly at no great distance, calling out, 'Jan Coo! Jan Coo!'

The men shouted in reply, at which the voice ceased. Lights were fetched and they searched around the spot, but no traces of anyone could be seen, so after spending some further time in calling, but without obtaining any response, they re-entered the house, not knowing what to think.

The next night came; the men were gathered around the hearth as before, when the boy rushed in to say that the voice could again be heard. Up jumped the men, and running to the spot to which

29

they had gone the previous night, listened intently. Out of the stillness of the night came the voice, calling again, 'Jan Coo! Jan Coo!' They looked at one another, but stayed silent, waiting until the voice should be heard once more before replying. And once again upon the night air came the cry 'Jan Coo! Jan Coo!' at which they gave a lusty shout, but waited in vain for any response. All was silent, and after trying again by repeated calls to get an answer from the mysterious visitor, they once more sought the warmth of the chimney corner.

''Tis the pisgies, I'll warn,' said an old man as he settled down on his low seat by the fire. 'I've heard mun say that you can't tell mun, when they be calling, from a Christian.'

'Eess, that's what that is, vor sartin; an' us had better let 'em bide, an' not meddle wi'em,' said another, so they all decided to take no further notice of the strange voice, should it be heard again. And heard again it was. Not a night passed but, as soon as the men were gathered around the fire after their evening meal, the mysterious voice again rang through the valley – 'Jan Coo! Jan Coo!'

The winter had nearly passed away, and the people at the farm were looking forward to the fast-approaching spring, when the lad, with one of the labourers, was mounting the slope that stretched from the house down to the river. It was dusk and they were returning home to their supper, having finished their work for the day. Suddenly the voice was heard in Langamarsh Pit, on the other side of the river, calling as before, 'Jan Coo! Jan Coo!' The boy instantly shouted in reply, when, instead of the calls ceasing as on the occasions when the men had replied to them, they were heard again, 'Jan Coo! Jan Coo!' Once more the lad shouted, and again there came the same cry, this time louder than before.

'I'll go and see what 'tis,' exclaimed the boy; and before his companion could attempt to dissuade him from it, he had started to run down the hill towards the river. The many boulders in its rocky bed made crossing places at certain points – when the stream was not swollen with the rains – known to those living in the vicinity, and towards one of these the boy made his way. His companion watched him but a short distance, for in the deepening twilight he was speedily lost to view, but as the man continued his ascent of the hill the voice still came from Langamarsh Pit, 'Jan Coo! Jan Coo!' Again as he approached the farmhouse, he could hear it, and as he neared the door the sounds still rang through the valley, 'Jan Coo! Jan Coo!' Gaining the threshold, he paused before entering, with his hand holding the string which raised the latch, and listened for the voice once more. It had ceased.

He waited but no sound broke the stillness of the evening, and seeking the kitchen he told what had happened to those gathered there, who wondered what the lad would have to tell them when he came back. Hour after hour passed away. The boy did not come. The men went down to the river and called him by name, but they received no reply; they waited expecting him to return, but he didn't appear, and as no news of him was ever obtained, and the mysterious voice ceased its nightly calls, they came to the conclusion that he had been spirited away by pixies.

A Huccaby Courting

From *Tales of the Dartmoor Pixies* by William Crossing

On the left bank of the River Dart, just above Hexworthy Bridge, stands Huccaby Farmhouse, where, several years ago, the presiding genius of the dairy was a buxom lass whose attractions were not unheeded by the youthful swains of the neighbourhood.

But the rivalry for the smiles of the damsel was of a friendly nature, and the passion of her many admirers, though in all probability not deficient in ardour, was not of too deep-rooted a character. They were able to bear up against the disappointment of losing her, for when it at last became known that Tom White, of Postbridge, was the favoured suitor, the others took a very philosophical view of the matter, and instead of rushing off straightaway to hang themselves from the nearest tree – or, as trees are scarce objects on the moor, taking a fatal plunge in the waters of the Dart – they thought no more about it but quietly left Tom with the field to himself.

Postbridge is nearly five miles from Huccaby, and as his farm work would not permit him to visit the lady of his love by day, he was forced to content himself with seeing her in the evening, when labour was over. After a hearty evening meal – for Tom did not believe in making love on an empty stomach – he would set out to walk the five miles like a man, and at the end of his meeting with the fair maiden he would trudge back again to his home. A walk of ten miles after a day spent in labour is an undertaking that many men would shrink from; but what is it to a man in love? And the plucky way in which Tom accomplished it, several evenings a week, proved the ardour of his passion. Boldly would he set forth from his home and walk over Lakehead Hill and by the rugged rocks of Bellaford [Bellever] Tor was rendered light and easy by the anticipation of the blissful time in store for him, and his journey back was made cheerful by his recollection of it.

One would suppose that a man who could look lightly upon a walk of this kind would be so firm in his determination to win the young lady's hand that nothing would turn him from it. But alas! It was not to be so. One summer night Tom had stayed rather later than usual, and as he strode onward, after mounting the slope behind the house, he saw that the stars were beginning to pale before the coming dawn.

He walked rapidly, for he began to think that he would hardly get to bed before the hour when he must rise to go to work, and he was anxious to get home as soon as he could.

Plodding onward, Tom soon reached the slope of Bellaford Tor. As he passed by the walls of the new-takes and approached the tor itself, he fancied he heard sounds of merry voices in the distance. Once or twice he paused to listen, but the sounds were so faint, and the probability of anyone being about at that early hour in such a spot so slight, that he came to the conclusion he had mistaken the sighing of the wind for voices, and pressed on his way.

And now the rocks of the tor began to rise dimly before him, assuming in that uncertain light strange and fantastic shapes. The ground over which he was passing was strewn with granite blocks, and he had to proceed more cautiously. Arrived at the tor, he was threading his way through the scattered rocks with the intention of passing on one side of it, when suddenly sounds similar to those he had previously heard struck upon his ear, but so plainly that he knew he was labouring under no delusion.

Before he could look around him to discover where the sounds came from, their volume increased tenfold, and it was evident that a very merry party was somewhere close at hand. Now it flashed into his mind that he had approached a pixy gathering, and stepping at that instant round a huge granite boulder, he came upon a strange and bewildering sight.

On a small level piece of velvety turf, entirely surrounded by boulders, a throng of little creatures were assembled, dressed in most fantastic costumes. A great number of them had joined hands, and were dancing merrily in a ring, while many were perched upon the rocks around, and all were laughing and shouting with glee. Poor Tom was frightened beyond measure, and knew not whether it was better to proceed or try to retreat. If he could steal away unobserved he might be able to pass on the opposite side of the tor, and this he decided to do. But no sooner had he made up his mind than the little folks spotted him, and, instantly forming a ring round him, danced more furiously than ever.

As they whirled around, Tom was forced to turn round with them; although they danced so rapidly that he was utterly unable to keep up with their frantic movements. Each one, too, was joining in the elfin chorus as loud as his little lungs would enable him, and although they danced and sang with all their might they never seemed to tire.

In vain Tom called upon them to stop – his cries only causing the pixies to laugh the merrier – while they seemed to have no intention whatever of stopping their antics. Tom's head began to swing round; he put out his arms wildly, his legs felt as if they would give way under him; yet he could not avoid spinning round in a mad whirl. He would have given anything to stop, and endeavoured in vain to throw himself on the grass; the mad gallop still continued, and poor Tom was compelled to take his part in it.

In the height of the din, the sun began to rise above the ridge of Hameldon, and at the first sight of it the noise suddenly ceased, the little folk instantly vanished among the crevices of the rocks, and

Tom found himself lying alone on the moor.

Plucking up his courage, he made his way towards home as fast as he was able, devoutly hoping he might reach it without encountering any more pixies. This he fortunately did, and got to rest without delay.

But alas! The pixies had done more harm than merely worrying a poor mortal; they were the means of the buxom damsel of Huccaby losing her lover. Poor Tom was so frightened at his night's adventure that he made a vow, that he would never go courting any more – and he kept it. It is probable there were people who were ready to doubt if Tom White ever saw the pixies at all, and were prepared to assign as a reason for his belief that he did so, the probability that he had consumed something a little stronger than water, before leaving his lady-love, and this would account for the spirits getting into his head.

Be that as it may, Tom stoutly declared it was all as he said, and resolutely stuck to his determination of avoiding the fascinations of the fair sex in future.

Threshing for Farmers

From *Tales of the Dartmoor Pixies* by William Crossing

A small farmer once lived on the moor, who was so very poor that he had as much as he could do to keep himself and his family from starving.

He cultivated a few fields which had been reclaimed from the waste but the crops were seldom of much value.

One day, on approaching his barn, he heard sounds of laughter and merriment proceeding from within. Going cautiously to the door, he put his ear to the crevice and heard what seemed to be a company of little people busily engaged in threshing corn. After having listened for some time, he stepped quietly away and remained at work at the other end of the yard until he judged the pixies – for such he knew the little labourers to be – had finished their task. Then, proceeding to the barn once more, he was mightily pleased at discovering what the merry little troop of workers had accomplished for him. They had threshed a goodly quantity of his corn, and having relieved him of the trouble of doing it himself, had given him time for the rest of his work, and by nightfall he found there was as much done as would have taken him nearly two days to perform by himself.

This put him in good humour, and he decided not to go to the barn on the next morning, but to let the pixies have it all their own way. He carried out this resolution, and it wasn't until late afternoon that he approached the barn. On entering it he was met by the same pleasing sight as on the preceding morning. Curiosity now took possession of his mind, and he began to think he should like to see the little people at work. He knew it would be necessary to exercise caution, so he decided on going very early to the barn on the following morning, and waiting in hiding for the arrival of the pixies. This he did, and after a time was delighted at seeing the troop of little people run merrily into the barn, some of them carrying flails (or 'dreshels' as they are called in Devonshire) on their shoulders. Soon all was bustle and noise. The strokes of the flails resounded on the floor, and peals of laughter rang through the old barn, as the active little goblins bent to their task.

The farmer looked on with amazement from his station behind the straw, eagerly gazing at the astonishing scene before him. On a sudden, one of the pixies – a sharp, pert-looking fellow – dropped his flail and cried out in a shrill voice, 'I twit, you twit.' The others looked up, and threw down their flails too. Now the farmer, although he had not been discovered, imagined he had been, and remembering that once the pixies learn they are overlooked they never return to the spot again, was filled with vexation, and as the pert little fellow on the floor once more raised his tiny voice and called out, 'I twit, you twit,' he rushed forth in a temper exclaiming, 'I'll twit 'ee!' upon which the pixies immediately vanished, and never came near his barn any more.

There is an alternative ending to this tale, in which the farmer leaves well alone, instructs his labourers to do likewise, and rapidly makes his fortune.

The Fairies' Ointment, as Nurse Warren told it

From *A Book of the West* by Sabine Baring Gould

You have many times asked me to tell you about the fairies' ointment. Now I don't suppose you will believe me, but I have heard Granny say that a very long time ago there were Pixies scattered all over the country. The Pixies were good and kind to some people, but to others they would play all sorts of tricks. You must never spy on a Pixy, for they would be sure to pay you out if you did. Now the story I am going to tell you was told to me by my grandmother, who died in her eighty-seventh year, and she heard it from her mother. So this all happened before there was any King George. Granny used to say that she believed it was when there was a King Henry, who had a number of wives.

There was a wonderfully clever midwife, called Morada, who lived a little way out of Holne village, close to Dartmoor. You know in those days doctors were not so plentiful as they be now, nor so clever; so the people all around used to send for Nurse Morada. Now she was a widow woman and a foreigner. Folks did say she was a witch, and a sight of money she got, for folks was afraid to offend her.

One night just before harvest Nurse had gone to bed early, for it was a dark, dismal evening, likely for a thunderstorm and Nurse was much afraid of lightning.

She had not been long asleep when she was awakened by such a clatter at the door as if it was being broken down, and it was thundering and lightning frightful. Nurse was greatly frightened, but lay still, hoping the knocking would cease, but it only got worse and worse. At last she rose and opened the window, when she saw by the lightning flashing, which almost blinded her, a little man sitting on a big horse, hammering at the door.

'Come down, woman,' he said; 'my wife is ill, and wants you.'

'Do you think I'm mad?' she called out. 'I would not go out for the queen herself such a night as this,' and was going to shut the window.

'Stop!' he cried out; 'will you come with me for ten golden guineas?'

Now this was a sight of money in those days, and Nurse was very greedy for money; so she told the man to wait, and she would be dressed as soon as possible.

The man jumped down from his horse, and pointing to a shed said two words in a foreign language, whereupon the horse cleverly walked in out of the rain. The man entered the house, and when Nurse saw him she was that frightened she almost fainted away. He was not old at all, but a very handsome young man. He was small, to be sure, but he looked a real little gentleman, with such beautiful fine clothes, and eyes that fairly looked through you. He laughed to see how frightened the woman was.

'Now listen to me,' he said in a voice as sweet as a thrush's, 'and be sure that if you do what I tell you, and never speak of what you may see or hear, no harm will happen to you, and I will give you ten guineas now and ten more when you return home. If you keep your promise all will be well, but if you do not I will punish you very severely. Now to show you what power I have, I tell you that although you say that you are a widow and call yourself Morada, that is not your name, for you never were married. Shall I tell you some more of your past life?'

'No, sir, no!' she called out. 'I will do all that you tell me.'

'That's right and sensible. Now the first thing I do is to blindfold you, and you must not try to take off the bandage from your eyes. Take these ten guineas and put them away.'

This the woman did, and hid them behind the mantelpiece. They both left the house, the woman locking the door. He took the woman behind him on the horse, and tied her with a strap round her waist. Away went the horse like the wind across the moor; Nurse thought from the time they took they must have gone pretty near as far as Lydford. When he got off from the horse he made sure that she had not moved the handkerchief. Unlocking a door, he led her up through a long passage, and, unlocking another door, pulled her inside.

'Now take off your handkerchief,' said he, and she found herself in a queer-looking place all lighted up with beautiful lamps. A little squint-eyed man came and said something the Nurse could not understand. The little gentleman then hurried Nurse off into another room, where, lying on a beautiful velvet bed, was the prettiest little lady anybody ever did see.

Well, before many hours there was a sweet little dot of a boy born. Then the gentleman brought the Nurse a box of ointment and told her to rub some over the baby's eyelids. When nurse had done so she put the box in her pocket and forgot all about it. This got her into great trouble, as I'll tell you about presently. Nurse stayed some days with the little lady, and got to love her very much, she was that kind and good. The little lady liked Nurse, and told her that she herself was a princess; that her husband was a prince; that they lived in a beautiful country where there was no frost or snow, and that they were fairies, not pixies. Her father was the king of all the fairies, and he was very angry because she ran away and married the prince, who was not of so high a rank as she was, although he was her cousin, and that to punish them he sent 'em both to Dartmoor for a year. That time was now up, and they were all going home in a few days.

The fairy prince took Nurse to her home blindfolded on the big horse, in the same way as he brought her there, and on parting gave her the other ten guineas as he had promised. The next morning Nurse was in a great quandary when she found the box of ointment in her pocket. 'Well,' she thought, 'he will be sure to come for this ointment, as they will all be going away to-morrow or the next day.'

Nurse stayed up all that night, but the prince did not come, and the next day and night passed without seeing him. Then Nurse felt certain that they were all gone, and had forgotten the ointment, and she could scarcely eat, drink, or sleep for thinking what virtue there might be in it.

When the fourth night had passed without his coming Nurse could wait no longer, but opened the box and rubbed in a little of the ointment on her left eye; but she only felt the eye prick and sting a bit, so the woman thought the ointment must be only good for fairy babies, and she went to bed quite satisfied.

'The next morning she thought she must have died and awakened up in another world. Everything about her looked as if it had grown ever so much. The cat, which always slept in her room, looked as large as a great dog. Then remembering the ointment, she covered her left eye, and all was as it used to be. The woman now got very frightened, and started off after breakfast to go to Ashburton to consult a friend of hers, a Mr Stranger, who was very clever about herbs.

As she walked along she would now and again cover up her right eye, and then everything would look so grand and beautiful; and looking up, she saw stars, although the sun was shining brightly, she could see that wonderfully far off. Now, she had not gone very far when suddenly the fairy prince, sitting on his horse, appeared before her.

'Good morning, sir,' she said, dropping a curtsy.

'Ah!' he cried, 'the ointment! Which eye do you see me with?'

'The left, sir.'

Instantly she felt something like a blow on that eye. The fairy prince vanished, and appeared again as the little man she had first seen.

'Nurse,' said he, 'you are blinded in your left eye as a punishment for having used the ointment. I am sorry, for you were kind to my wife. Here is a present she has sent you.'

He then gave her ten guineas, and she returned him the box. He then vanished. This is all the story that Granny told me about the fairy ointment.

The Hairy Hands

The road between Postbridge and Princetown, particularly the section by Cherrybrook Bridge and the former black powder factory of Powder Mills, is said to be haunted by an evil presence which manifests itself as a pair of huge and hairy hands. Reports of this phenomenon are surprisingly recent, dating only from the 1920s.

In 1921 Dr Helby, the Princetown Prison Doctor, was thrown from his motorcycle near Powder Mills and died from a broken neck. However, the two small girls in the machine's side car were thrown onto the verge and shaken, but little hurt. This tragic accident was related to Devon folklorist Theo Brown by Mrs Battiscombe, the widow of Helby's successor.

Further incidents occurred, including one in which a charabanc suddenly left the road and ran into a ditch. Fortunately, neither the driver nor the passengers were injured. Mrs Battiscombe went on to describe a further motorcycle accident on the same stretch of road, in which the young rider returned to his lodgings 'very white and shaken and saying he had had a most curious experience'. He is reported to have said 'he felt his hands gripped by two rough and hairy hands and every effort made to throw him off his machine.'

The *Daily Mail* got hold of these stories in the autumn of 1921 and sent down reporters to investigate. This provoked a lively correspondence in the press, in which thought-forms, elementals and vengeful prehistoric inhabitants loomed large. Publicity reached such a pitch that the authorities felt impelled to investigate the road and find a rational explanation for these accidents. They declared the camber of the road was at fault and repaired it.

Theo Brown went on to relate how, a few years later, when she was still a child, she stayed with her family in a caravan near Powder Mills, close by the haunted road. She enjoyed the fine weather and playing with the farm children and their boat in the Cherrybrook, unaware until years later of her mother's terrifying experience. One night, Theo's mother woke suddenly with a deep sense of malaise, convinced she had seen the hairy hand clawing its way up the caravan window to attack her sleeping husband. However, the hairy hand retreated after she made the sign of the cross and prayed fervently. Ever after, she refused to walk that part of the moor alone.

Since then, there have been no further reports of the hairy hands.